Angels all Around Us

Written by:
Larry S. Glover

Illustrated by:
Mai Kemble

Published by:
Childlike Faith Children's Books

This book is dedicated to children who believe in angels,
and that angels are all around us.

©Larry S. Glover 2020
All Rights Reserved. This book, or parts, thereof, may not be reproduced
in any form without permission from the author or publisher.

Published by Childlike Faith Children's Books
2012 Wages Way
Jacksonville, FL 32218
Childlikefaithchildrensbooks.com

Author: Larry S. Glover
Illustration: Mai Kemble
Production: ABC Book Publishers, Inc.
Graphic Design: Jeanine Quinn
Editor: Kimberly Benton

Print ISBN: 978-1-7348268-5-2
Ebook ISBN: 978-1-7355149-1-8
Library of Congress Control Number: 2020945142
Printed in the United States of America

10 9 8 7 6 5 4 3 2 1

God has set his *Angels* to watch over us.
They will be with us wherever we go.
They will catch us with their hands
and we won't get hurt if we
hit our foot on a stone.

Psalm 91:11-12

Angels are all around us.

What do they do?
They *listen* to God's voice
and watch over
me and you.

There is an angel that is with us and given to us at birth.

They are right beside us while we live here on earth.

Some people say that angels are **TALL**, **BIG** and **STRONG**. But they can also be gentle enough to sing us a song.

Sometimes, Angels are there to help us when we play and fall.

There are some angels that can hear us, and come when we call.

Angels are at work and are here to do God's will. There are also angels at work to help us with the way we feel.

Angels are all around us
and they watch us every day.

They can also lead and guide us when we go the wrong way.

There are *Angels* that come to help us when we are in need.

They come with **LOVE** and *kindness* especially when there are people to feed.

There are Angels that come to help us with the things we need.

I will tell you all about these angels as you continue to read.

Healing *Angels* are here as we live from day to day.

They are here because **God loves us**, and they bless us in God's own way.

The helper Angel can do almost anything.
They go around the earth and bring God's blessings.

The peace Angel is with us each and every day; helping us find the rest we need in each and every way.

The star *Angel* is there to watch us as our dreams come true.

If you **talk** to this angel, he will **listen** to you.

There are messenger Angels that come from heaven to us on earth.

They tell us what God said so that we hear it first.

We have Michael the Archangel who is there to defend.
He helps us to be **STRONG**
and he can help us to **WIN.**

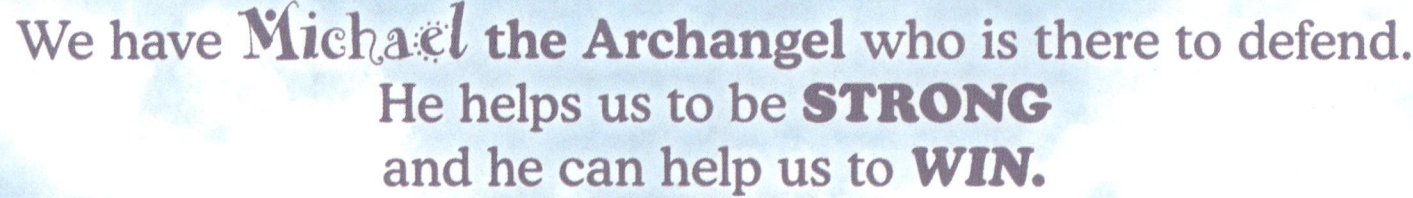

The **Archangel Gabriel** is always busy and working very hard.

He can *lead* us, *guide* us and brings blessings from **God**.

The **Archangel Urial**, is called the angel of light and day.

If you are ever feeling *lost* - he can *show you the way.*

The **Archangel** *Ariel* is there to remind us of –
FAITH, HOPE and **LOVE**,
but most of all **TRUST**.

The **Archangel Haniel** is the angel that is in charge of joy.

She can fill us with **God's love** for every girl and boy.

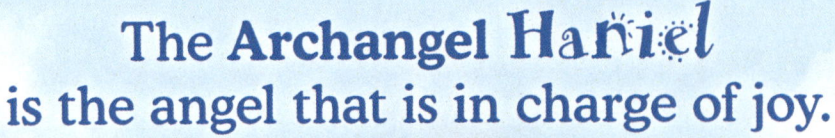

We have learned about *Angels*, and all that they can do.

I hope you will remember that angels are ALWAYS with you.

Be kind to Angels and they will be kind to you. They help us with sharing and caring between me and you.

When has an Angel helped you?

Archangel Fun Facts

Ariel – The Archangel Ariel's name means 'lion or lioness of God' Ariel is the patron saint of animals and the environment.

Ariel assists in healing injured animals working closely with Archangel Raphael in these endeavors.

Gabriel – Gabriel's name means "God is my strength" or "man of God".

Most famously, he announced to Mary the coming birth of Jesus.

Haniel – Archangel Haniel is known as the angel of joy. She works to direct people who are searching for fulfillment to God, who is the source of all joy.

Haniel "brings harmony and balance wherever she goes" and "reminds you to find fulfillment from within rather than trying to find happiness from outside yourself.

Michael – Christians saw the Archangel Michael as a protector *(someone who defends and helps)* and the leader of the army of God against the forces of evil.

The name Michael means, "Who is like God." In the Bible, he is called "one of the chief princes" (Daniel 10:13) and "the great prince" (Daniel 12:1)

Raphael – He is known in various religions as an angel who does acts of healing. The name Raphael means "It is God who heals", "God Heals", "God, Please Heal". Raphael is an angel in the Bible.

He is the patron saint (taking care of) the young people, shepherds; sick people and travelers.

Uriel – Uriel's name means "God is my light" or "fire of God") is an archangel in Jewish and Christian traditions.

RESOURCES:
Raphael (archangel) Facts for Kids. *Kiddle Encyclopedia.*
Gabriel Facts for Kids. *Kiddle Encyclopedia.*
Uriel Facts for Kids. *Kiddle Encyclopedia.*
Michael (archangel) Facts for Kids. *Kiddle Encyclopedia.*

https://www.beliefnet.com/inspiration/angels/8-biblical-facts-about-archangel-michael
https://www.beliefnet.com/inspiration/angels/galleries/the-7-archangels-and-their-meanings
https://www.learnreligions.com/how-to-recognize-archangel-haniel-124304

THE KIDS EMPOWERMENT SERIES
Order other books by Larry S. Glover:

Little Prayers That Work

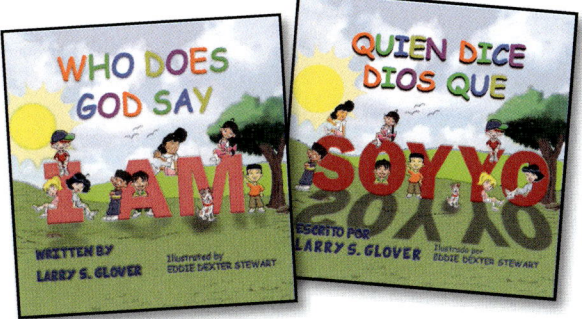
Who Does God Say I Am

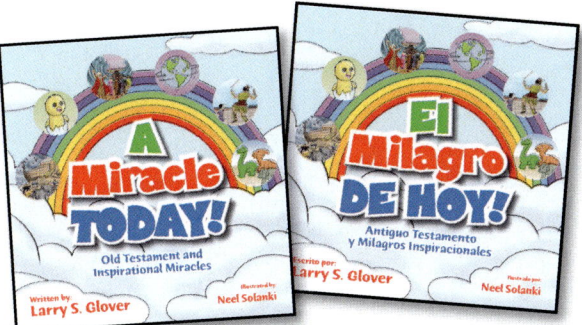
A Miracle Today – Old Testament

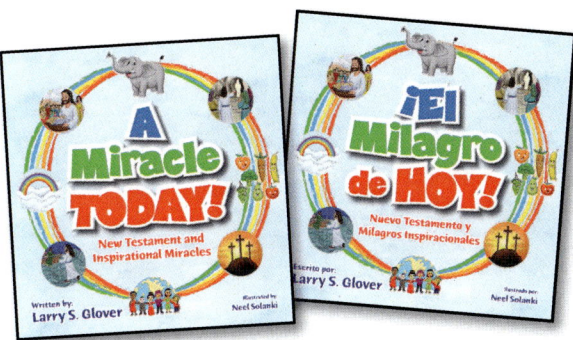
A Miracle Today – New Testament

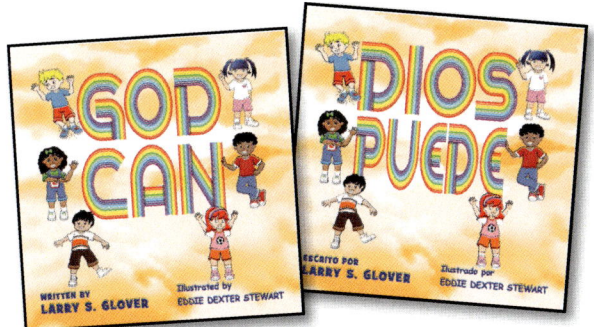
GOD CAN

Angels All Around Us

Coming Soon:
A Place Where We Can Go
God is Love

Available in English and Spanish
on Amazon.com
www.childlikefaithchildrensbooks.com

THE KID'S VALUE SERIES

Order other books by Larry S. Glover:

Available in English and Spanish.

Be Good

Be Kind

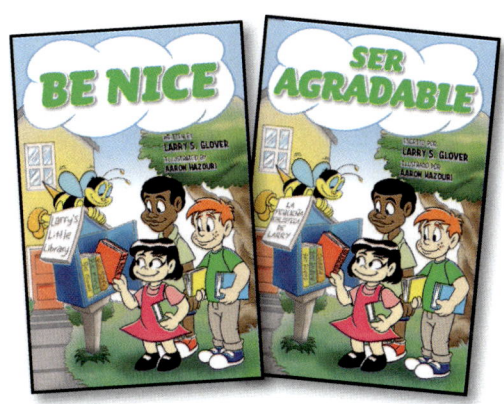
Be Nice

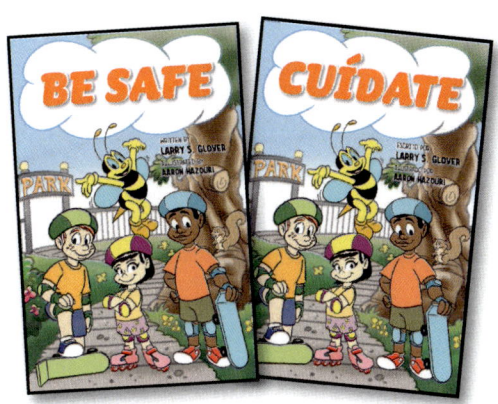
Be Safe

www.childlikefaithchildrensbooks.com

Made in the USA
Middletown, DE
16 June 2024